# STOP
## YOUR TODDLER'S
# TANTRUMS

THE MOTHER'S GUIDE TO
FINDING JOY IN PARENTING

SUSAN JUNGERMANN

Cover Design: Nakita Duncan

Editing: Emily Tuttle

Author's photo courtesy of: Britt Lakin

*For Oliva and Jaxon,*
*my greatest honor*
*is being your mother.*

# CONTENTS

# 1

# SO BURNT OUT

*"Burn-out is a bone-tired,*
*soul-tired, kind of exhaustion."*
*-J. Pennebaker*

## The Self-Loathing Mother

You wanted *these* children more than anything. They are the loves of your life, and when they sleep, you look at pictures of them. You can't imagine being away from them because it would feel like someone took your heart out. But, you desperately feel like you need a vacation. You feel failure and guilt. Guilt that you don't sing enough or dance enough or smile enough. Failure because, even though you've given up your entire self-identity, your child is far from behaved, and people notice. What is the price tag of a behaved child, because you couldn't have made a bigger sacrifice than your whole self?

You're tired. This is not as easy or as magical as you thought it would be. You didn't understand the self-sacrifice you were making when you gave up your own identity to help someone else grow theirs. You carry a baby in your front pouch and chase a three-year-old that feels more like a feral cat these days. Your back is aching, your hair is a mess, you're lucky if you've found clean yoga pants to put on this morning. This day will be just like all of the days – a cloudy collection of toddler screams, baby cries, and messes that interrupt your ever-present thoughts of "if only I were a better mom."

It wasn't always this way; your toddler was once sweet, and you're not sure if you've spoiled him into awfulness or if he managed his way there himself. He used to listen, and you felt like your connection was unbreakable. While he discovered the world from your arms, you thought life would never be more perfect. It's complicated now. A baby sister has joined your tribe. Your parents live close by. Your husband travels for work. You thought having one baby was a challenge. Then, one day you woke up and your sweet baby was a rough, rowdy, very challenging toddler.

Your toddler has decided that this would be a good time to give up naptime. Now you don't even have a moment in the day to rejuvenate or refresh. You do better with order and organization, but instead you have one half-finished project after another in every room. There are toys all over the place. The new baby's dirty clothes are on the counter. Dishes are in the sink and on the table still from breakfast. It's 11:00 AM, and despite your best efforts, you have had two events with your toddler that made him melt to the floor. First, his milk wasn't the right temperature, and then, he wanted to stay outside, but it was time to feed the baby, so you had to come inside.

Your own sleep is no longer refreshing; it's a time of self-deprecation about why you can't figure motherhood out. Billions of women have come before you, and here you are, messing up these children. You yell all day. You want to be kind and have good intentions and certainly want what's best for your children, but to make that actually all come true, in the heat of battle, feels impossible. You know sleep is best for you, but it is also the only moment of quiet you have in a day that seems impossibly long and unending.

You've had a successful career and a degree. You are capable and funny and passionate. Well, at least, you thought you were. You're questioning everything because isn't this what you've been training for your whole life? But this is the hardest job you've ever had, and you feel worse about yourself than ever before.

You don't remember what fun is. You watch other people and families carefully, study them. It seems like they are having fun. It seems like they are enjoying their children. You can't even remember what you like to do for fun. Your hobbies are long gone and forgotten. Your hobbies are now naming princesses, reading books, and stacking blocks, and that's on a good day. You don't even remember what you like to do for fun as a family. Is it even fun to take a toddler anywhere? It just feels like more work and less help in a less toddler-friendly environment. At least at home, you've barricaded enough doorways that you feel you can sit down for tea without being on stand-by.

I know you hate it when other people watch you interact with your child. It makes you feel more inadequate than you already feel. No matter what you try, the reaction you get from your child is not what you expect. He screams at the top of his lungs, whether it is in pleasure or disgust. He flails about, possessed with glee or anger. You want to calm him so you can help the others around you feel better, so they are not inconvenienced by your child. You wonder what they are thinking as you watch them watch you, like you're putting on a performance for an audience. You think to yourself, "He must be worse than their children were," or, "I wish I could control this wild child." The more you push towards calming him, the more excitable he gets. The more excitable he gets, the more frustrated you become. That's why it's easier to stay home. The reactions from other people make you feel worse about yourself, and right now, you already feel like you have an empty corner.

You didn't know you were going to feel so alone. Your husband is there, but he doesn't go through the same things you go through. You can't really talk to him about it, because he just assumes you're not disciplining enough or you're not strict enough. When you try to talk to him, it's hard not to take it personally because it's so personal! He's at work all day, he drives home in a quiet car, and he talks to adult people with whom he has dynamic relationships. You get yelled at about milk temperature and how socks feel. You are just not in the same place of understanding.

The relationship between your husband and toddler is also complex. Everything that goes right when he is watching your toddler, he assumes he has created. Everything that goes wrong is a combination of your child's bad listening and your bad parenting, or your lack of "putting your foot down." He thinks your toddler might not be so unruly if you provided more structure or gave him more time-outs, or perhaps tried spanking. I know you liked him more as a person when you were dating.

How long should you let this go on? What will feeling like this do to you? You can already tell you've changed as a person. You feel like your sparkle has faded. Sometimes in the morning, when you are getting out of bed, you start counting down the minutes until you can get back in bed. You feel so tired and lonely. You've gained weight. You've withdrawn more from going places. What will it be like in two years, when your baby is a toddler? The thought of even having a third baby right now is terrifying, but once that all seemed like part of the dream.

Can you imagine not feeling like this? Can you imagine waking up and being excited to start your day? Excited to greet your toddler, ready for a day of adventure? How different would your life feel if you had the ability to make it feel fun, exciting, and in control? Think about going to the store and not worrying about what people were going to do or say, because you already knew that everything would work out, that your toddler would behave when you went places. Think about how easy it would be if you were able to predict the behavior of your toddler. Your life wouldn't feel like a series of reactions to natural disasters, but a flow of easy, fun, and carefree days. Sound impossible? I'm telling you, it isn't! I have been exactly where you are. It is time for you to start living the life you deserve!

The problem with feeling this way is that it's hard to remember that it's fleeting. It's not everlasting, and soon you'll want these days back, I promise. However, when you feel so stuck, it's hard not to let the feeling of "stuckness" rule the day. It feels like toddlerville will go on forever, and it feels like you will be lost forever, which makes you feel like you could possibly feel unhappy forever.

If you are reading this book, you are reading it for a reason. You are meant to be here, right now. I want to let you know that our club is a large one: the "Guilty Moms" club, the "I Wish I Was a Better Mom" club, the "I Suck at Mothering" club, the "Why Does my Toddler Hate me?" club. Whatever you want to name it, there is a large following of underpaid, overworked women who, just like you, pay their dues day in and day out. Mama, it is time for you to stop paying your dues and get your life back!

# 2

## THERE'S GOT TO BE AN EASIER WAY

*"You have to keep breaking your heart until it opens"*
*-Rumi*

I know exactly how you are feeling. In between moments of being yelled at, tripping over toys, telling the dog to go lay down, and picking up a crying baby, you are wondering how this became your life. How a battle for keeping shoes on became the difference between showing up on time or twenty minutes late. How taking a shower became a luxury. How it feels like your time is valueless. I was also playing by that set of rules, along with every other mother of young children I spoke to. I had to go deep into the depths of despair before I could find my way to freedom. This is how that journey started.

## In a Panic

In 2010, I was managing a Goddard School, and felt like it was the perfect fit for me. I had a background in child development, as well as business operations, and this job combined those skills perfectly. We lived in Dublin, Ohio, an affluent suburb in the northwest of Columbus. I was proud to represent a respected preschool in a nice area. I had started working there when I was eight months pregnant with our son, and our daughter, Olivia, was eighteen months. It felt heartbreaking as a mother to watch Olivia transition from a child that had spent every waking moment with me to a child that would now be in a group care setting. Although she was in the building with me, I learned quickly to not let her see me. Drop offs in the morning were hard and being only feet from her classroom those first days, I would hear her crying for hours at a time.

Soon after, our son Jaxon was born, and after a six-week maternity leave, he started coming to the school, too. I didn't realize what effect infant group care would have on him. His baby years were filled with ten-day fevers and breathing treatment after breathing treatment. I also didn't realize I was about to start the fight of my life.

I soon got into a rhythm with the school. The owners, who were kind and supportive, hired their brother-in-law to help support me. We had a great rapport and were able to really fill up the school. I really felt like I was where I was meant to be, professionally.

Around this time, unexpectedly, I started suffering from debilitating panic attacks. The first one happened at a Target with my daughter, Olivia, with me. I felt a sharp pain in my left arm, and I instantly thought I was having a heart attack. I was actively thinking I was dying, and I couldn't imagine my babies growing up without me. I was facing death, and I felt like I hadn't really lived. That day was a life changer. I did anything and everything I could to prevent future panic attacks, but nothing worked.

Some nights I would crawl up the stairs with a small baby, while flanking my toddler. I was too dizzy and nauseous to stand, and the sweat would be pouring off of me. I would put Jaxon in his crib and put Olivia in bed with me, then lay there and try to count fan rotations to prevent my death.

I always felt overwhelmed. The amount of work involved with keeping up with two small children was overwhelming enough, but I also had a full-time job, and I didn't feel any support from my husband. He worked full time and went to school. I have often wondered if it was easier for him to go to school than it was to be at home. He started "collecting" things pretty intensely in this period of our lives. I didn't notice at first. He had always had a general lack of organization, but this became accumulation on top of disorganization. If he found a container or empty pill bottle, he wanted to repurpose it. If he had one hammer, then he had four. He had countless hobbies, each one lasting as long as he had enough money to buy another hobby. That accumulation became a heavy burden on me.

It was about this time that I walked into work and was told the school was being sold. I would meet the new owners at 11:00 AM that same day, since I was part of the deal, a deal that had been brewing behind my back for months. I immediately felt betrayed. I thought I was part of a team that valued me and cared about me, but at the end of the day, I was just a piece of their puzzle.

I met the new owners for lunch that day, then they came to the school that evening and I personally introduced them to every family with a smile. But, the new owner was pretty awful. It started bad, ended worse, and to say our values were misaligned is an understatement. I ended up getting fired, something that has never happened to me before. It shook me to the core.

## A Story of Broken Legs

I was reeling from being fired, which manifested as me being in hiding for almost two years. I didn't want to see anyone. I was embarrassed, and I felt purposeless. Eventually, I decided that I would watch babies in my home, and had some families from the Goddard school reach out. On my first day of officially watching children at home, I got a panicked call from Carl, my husband. He was at the Riverside hospital. He had fallen and shattered his heal, and they were taking him in to surgery.

I'm not sure what I was expecting from a shattered heel, but he had a multi-day hospital visit. He was at home for several months for rehab and pain. He would start walking on it and it would be intolerable so he would start back at square one with another try at surgery.

That same year, my brother had gotten me and my sister tickets to a Miranda Lambert concert for Christmas. During a set, I got up to go to the restroom and hyperextended my knee while walking, which resulted in a broken tibia plateau and a torn LCL. I had broken bones nine times before and knew immediately it was broken. I thought, "Please, don't let this be happening." Security came to help and went to get my sister. They tried to get me to stand up, and I told them I just needed an ambulance. The ambulance brought me to Grant Medical Center, where a broken leg was confirmed, and they sent me to a room. I would be having surgery early the next morning.

Over the next months, Carl and I took turns having surgery. We were lucky, in a sense, that we were both home and able to support each other through our individual surgeries. He ended up getting five surgeries in total and I ended up getting four. His fifth and final surgery was a below the knee amputation.

Looking back, I have wondered what he was thinking, as he sat for weeks at a time in the chair appropriately named "La-Z Boy." I wondered if he saw me, also mobile by wheel chair only, parenting one day post-op while unloading the dishwasher. Every night, I would back my broken body up the stairs to the wheel chair waiting to welcome me at the top, so I could tuck my kids in. Every morning, I would hop back down stairs and welcome the families that relied on me to watch their little ones so they could go to work. He would still be in his lazy boy. After the amputation, I understood his need for grief and processing time. The two and a half years leading up to the amputation allowed plenty of time for resentment and feeling betrayed for him leaving me high and dry again, with small children. I again felt alone, overwhelmed by his chaos and ever-growing piles of accumulation and, again, felt purposeless. I hated my life.

## A Long Dark Depression

I was fat, unable to get around in a productive way. My body would break easily. I lacked energy and any kind of real-life force that made it enjoyable to get up in the morning. I remember watching commercials about "depression hurting" and thinking "Man, is that the understatement of the year." Depression for me feels like being alone in a dark tunnel filled with syrup, with a tiny pinhole of light at the end to guide you, and anyone that comes in to help you or talk to you just covers up the pinhole of light. It is a completely joyless experience.

I was laying on the couch, hoping to get through the day, and mask any nonfeeling state for my children. I had turned on *The Incredibles*, and as I watched Mr. Incredible pull into his driveway, I recognized what he was feeling. The insinuation was, "Is this all life has for me? This tiny plot of land with this tiny driveway in my tiny car living a completely ordinary life?" You could tell he felt completely underwhelmed and a shadow of his former self. It was exactly how I was feeling. I felt a disappointment that this was all life had to offer.

Everyday felt like Groundhog Day. I was lonely, tired, and joyless. The garage was filled with so much junk by this point, every day that I had to take my kids to school, I had to walk over rocks to put the car seats in the car. Every day, the same thoughts went through my head. "How could the lazy boy care so little about me that he lets my broken body climb over rocks with car seats?" My thoughts perpetuated my emotions and attitude towards him.

## Finding My Own Way Out

I had to start doing something differently. I couldn't continue to live this way, because each day was a hundred years long, and it was torture. My days consisted of babies screaming at me and each other, regardless of what I tried. I had tried all of my baby tricks, but still, they were never all happy at the same time. This resulted in self-deprecation and self-pity. I had to start doing something differently.

At that time, I was watching five babies, and my schedule was very busy. I had to figure out something I could do for me, while I was with the babies. At first, I just started stretching.

It felt natural and like something my body needed. I would stretch every day, and it started to make my body feel better. Then, I started eating differently. I cut all sugar out of my diet. I didn't obsess about it, and it wasn't a shade of grey decision; it was black and white. If it had sugar, I wasn't eating it. After that, the correlation between sugar and carbs became pretty obvious. It got to a point where I was eating proteins, vegetables, and fats and would try to go as long as I could before I would eat again. I made my relationship with food about staying alive, not enjoyment. I stopped attaching feelings to food and started to understand the feelings were from me, not from the food. It was a game changer. I lost weight every week, sometimes ten pounds at a time.

When I started to feel better physically, I started to feel better emotionally. My internal world was lighter. I could feel emotion again. My days were easier. The babies that I had previously spent day in and day out reacting to like a pin ball were now reacting to me differently. The daily tantrums and screaming had significantly slowed despite my previous best efforts. So, why the sudden change? Was I just coping better? Was this good planning? Positive thinking? How were the toddlers reacting in my outer world to what was happening in my inner world?

I started to become very aware of our time together. If I was going to be at home, I was going to be the best "me at home" I could be. I always felt like I gave one hundred-percent of myself to the babies, but I needed to give one hundred-percent to myself first. Then, I could effectively give one hundred-percent of myself to the babies. That meant setting my external world up for success each day, planning ahead, creating effective schedules, and creating clear limits. That also meant I had some inner work to do each day. I needed to practice better self care, quiet my mind, and be clearer on my thoughts. After all the experiences I had with children and child development, I felt like I was at the very beginning of a new kind of understanding, and what I was understanding was going to be life changing.

It's time to make your life the wonderful life you should have, too! With a bit of planning and preparation and some self-love and care, you can be living the life of your dreams. Life is too short to waste it feeling unworthy or unvalued. You can find your worthiness within and I am going to show you where it is located. It is time to become the full you, the you that you are meant to be.

# 3

# PROCESS SNAPSHOT

*"Why do you want to stay in this prison*
*when the door is so wide open?"*
*- Rumi*

Remember those pictures that were popular back in the early 2000s? At first, when you looked at them, they were 2-D, but if you softened your gaze, the picture would jump out at you almost as if it were a whole new creation that you couldn't see before? Or, there's another type of picture that's almost two completely different pictures in one, and most often it's a picture that looks like something common. But, if you can train your brain to look at it a different way, there's something completely surprising that you would've never seen had you not been taught to look at it differently. Once you see it, however, you will never not see it again. Reading this book will be like that experience for some of you.

Sometimes, it will be a left brained experience, logical and practical, with seemingly simple concepts that can to be applied in everyday life. Other times, it will sound too simple or off the wall, and that's when I'll start to ask you to soften your gaze. What I'm asking from you, the reader, is to approach the book with an open mind. To look at it with a gaze that is softened so you can see the picture that pops out at you. To train your brain in a way that looks at things differently, that thinks about things differently and makes use of your right and left sides of the brain.

When I ask you to open up your mind, this is what I'm asking you to do. I'm asking you to consider all of everything you know as a belief that you have. All a belief is, is a thought that you continue to think. You could have a belief that heights are unsafe, and that thought can bring you fear. Just because that is your belief does not make it true. Our lives are based on our beliefs and our beliefs are ideas we pick up along the way, either programmed in us before the age of seven, an idea we got from an experience, or an idea we got from our perceptions.

## Conscious Vs. Subconscious Minds

Your brain is made up of two minds. You have what psychologists call the conscious mind, which controls short-term memory and the subconscious mind, which controls all long-term memory. These two minds learn and operate completely differently. When completing tasks, these two minds do different things for us.

Consider when you're walking down the street, and you're playing on your cell phone. The part of you that is playing on your cell phone is operated by the conscious mind. The part of you that keeps the "system" walking is the subconscious mind. The subconscious mind makes sure that it keeps us alive. It breathes for us, beats our hearts, keeps our body temperatures consistent, and has a rhythm that controls our sleep. It does everything in our bodies necessary to maintain a state of homeostasis. The subconscious mind operates without our thinking about it, while the conscious mind requires our thought. It controls the wanted behavior. The conscious mind does all day-to-day activities, such as talking on the phone, going grocery shopping, writing a check, cooking, etc. It is the thinking, creative mind.

The conscious mind learns through self-help books and a-ha moments. It can realize the truth and just start operating a new way. The subconscious mind must learn through hypnosis, where all of our beliefs came from before the age of seven. Even before you were born, your subconscious mind was learning. It was hearing music, feeling your mother's emotions in happiness and stress. If your mother was an addict, your subconscious learned the blood chemistry to deal with stress. All throughout your childhood, your subconscious took in information all around you, how people treated you and each other, and has been making determinations based on those references ever since. Before the age of seven, we were in a low frequency brain state called alpha. This enabled our subconscious brains to pick up on concepts around our environment. After the age of about seven, the subconscious closes off and the brain starts to operate at a higher frequency, so it is not so influenced by its environment.

The subconscious also learns through habituation. Some beliefs built through habits are learning the alphabet or how to drive a car. You practice and practice the skill until you can participate in the skill without "thinking" about it. We spend only about five-percent of our day in our conscious mind and ninety-five percent of our day in our subconscious mind. That's why it is so important to know what your true beliefs are.

## Your Beliefs

It is sometimes very difficult to know what beliefs you truly have. There are beliefs about money, self-worth, gender, the environment, success, education. You can look around your life and see where you have limiting beliefs. If you don't have as much money as you would like, you have a limiting belief about money. If you don't have the relationship you would like, you have a limiting belief about love or relationships. So, as you might see, you could have some self-limiting beliefs that you wouldn't know existed, and they could really be affecting your life.

Some ideas in this book may resonate with you, but, because of a belief, it may be limiting you from understanding. Continue to press on; the more you seek to understand, the easier it will become. What I know is, if you are reading this book, this message is for you. You would not have found this book or stumbled upon it if you were not supposed to be reading it. When you change the way you look at things, the things you look at start to change.

I really felt like I knew so much about child development. Afterall, most of my life has been spent around nurturing children. But I have learned the most about children in the last year, and it has really had nothing to do with children, specifically. What I have learned, I have applied personally, and the results have been non-fail, every single time. That said, it takes focus, determination, and a spirit of openness. You will get discouraged, but just keep trying. I have to remind myself every day of what I have learned, but it is well worth the commitment!

## Overview of Book

As you read this book, it is broken down into two sections. The first section of the book is about getting your external environment ready. It is more practical, everyday things that will certainly help you in managing life with a toddler. They will make sense and will be easy to implement. Like any new process, consistency is key.

We will go into detail about:

- Planning and activities
- How to transition from activities
- Routines
- Building effective schedules

The second section we will dive into your internal world. This is where I will ask you to keep an open mind and ask you to be excited about the process. This is where you can really make a lifelong difference in your life and in the lives of your children.

We will go into detail about:

- Discipline vs. Conscious Parenting through being present
- How to connect with a more authentic you
- Self-care and figuring out what's happening in your inner world

By working on your inner world and your outer world, you will have a clearer understanding of what is triggering your toddler. Consider your subconscious your angel, and whatever you tell it and make it truly believe, it will make sure it provides you in your life. So, starting right this minute, the negative self-talk has to go. Your subconscious is listening. Whatever you tell it, it will make sure it provides for you! Today, you are going to start to change your own story. In this story, you are the director.

# Part 1

---

# PREPARING YOUR EXTERNAL ENVIRONMENT

# 4

## PLANNING AND PREPARATION

*"Give a woman pain and she'll turn it into power.*
*Give that woman chaos and she'll create peace."*
*- r.h. Sin|XXll*

So many times, after my babies were tucked in their cribs for naptime, I'd look around the kitchen and wonder what had happened. I was frustrated, frazzled, frumpy, and tired. There was junk everywhere. Clothes and used diapers I had pulled off babies, food on the counter and the floor because the dog pulled the plate off the counter when I went upstairs. I felt like I was a hamster on a wheel. I could never "be done." My husband didn't understand, because he left work. I was stuck in my own private prison, physically and emotionally. I begrudgingly swept the floors, wiped the counters, loaded the dishwasher, skipped my own lunch in lieu of a load of laundry. In one short hour, the babies would be back up, my kids would be home from school, and my husband would be home. Everyone would destroy whatever desire I had to will myself to clean. I felt like an eighteen-wheeler would roll right over me and no one would notice. There had to be an easier way.

## Hamburger Stand Theory

Little did I know that when I worked at TGI Friday's, I would take so many life lessons with me. TGI Friday's training was built around a system of theories, so servers could better understand the "why" behind the way things were done. A particularly relevant theory for life in general was the "Hamburger Stand Theory." I have applied this theory to my life over and over. Maybe it's the name, or maybe it's the importance behind the name, but either way it has served me well.

The theory goes something like this. Adam and Eve, in the Garden of Eden, were setting up a Hamburger Stand. They cut some tomatoes, some lettuce, some onions, grilled some burgers, got some buns, grabbed some condiments, and off they went. Lots of creatures were interested in their burgers and before you knew it, Adam had to run off to pick and slice another tomato, which backed up the line a bit. No problem, the tomato situation was fixed. However, now that the tomatoes were resupplied, the lettuce had run out. Each time the team had to run and resupply, it was hard on everyone! It was hard on Adam and Eve, and it was hard on the creatures waiting in line, because they were hungry and impatient!

The next day, when Adam and Eve reopened their stand, they realized the value in the previous day's lesson. They really stocked their stand. They even put extra supplies in the bottom of the stand in case they ran out of their back-ups. They had a much better day in the Garden of Eden. The Hamburger Stand was so much more successful, because Adam and Eve had done the work ahead of time when they weren't busy, and it allowed their busy time to flow much more smoothly. As you can see, this theory can apply to any aspect of your life. I really want to break it down when it comes to toddlers.

Like creatures in the garden of Eden, toddlers are not equipped with an unlimited supply of attention or patience. Telling a toddler to wait is like telling spilled water not to move. Often times, when I had my own childcare in my home, I would have plenty of toys. I would rotate them a tremendous amount of times, but I was still running into boredom quickly, and transition times were awful. I began to take note of what was going on. At that time, I was watching a two, three, and four-year-old. Any time they got bored, they would attack each other, which obviously is not ideal. It was easy to determine a bored toddler is a bad toddler, and I didn't necessarily want to be an entertainer! I wanted to be an engager. I could not even leave the room to make lunch. Some activities were longer lived, like if they hadn't seen a toy in awhile, or if I had some newer toys, but I didn't have an unlimited budget for toys. I had to make something different work throughout the day.

The greatest challenge with toddlers is the ever-changing attention span. You don't want to be a full-time child entertainer, you want to be a child engager. You want activities that teach them to think, that make them use problem solving skills and fine motor skills. Activities that make them figure out one-to-one relationships, spatial awareness, and to see how things work and move. You want activities that they can work on independently or together in a group. You need activities that you can whip out that are premade, safe, and quickly picked up. The toy doesn't have to be new, they just need to be able to experience it differently. Toys don't have to be complicated or even considered "toys." For example, keep large Gold Peak Iced

Tea containers. Put two of the empty containers on the floor with two buckets-worth of ping pong balls. As they are putting the balls back in the container, they are also cleaning them up. This is an easy and quick activity, if you need to buy yourself about five to ten minutes.

## Quick, Easy Activities

You can make what I like to call "toddler activity bins." These are magic bins that, when they come out, you know you have a few minutes that you can get what you need done. These are activities they don't normally see. They don't have access to these, and they can't get them over and over. A few examples are:

- Ping pong balls and a bin of water with scoops
- Potting soil with dinosaurs, sticks, rocks, and leaves
- Potting soil and plastic bugs, leaves, sticks and rocks
- Fake flowers with potting soil, plastic bugs, leaves, sticks, and rocks
- String and beads with holes
- Construction paper and markers
- Ping pong balls and muffin tins
- Masking tape and cars, build road on floor
- Giant paper you can hang on the wall and let them draw on with markers
- Giant raw noodles and string
- Playdoh with hard rice mixed in it
- Blow up balloons and paper plates to hit the balloons back and forth
- Streamers, wrapping paper, and bows

- Collection of items from a nature walk and a magnifying glass
- Water with blue dye and water animals
- Spray bottle and construction paper
- Marker, coffee filter, and spray bottle
- Kids magazines that come in the mail
- Chalk and black construction paper

These are just a few examples using supplies you already have, or cheap supplies at the dollar store. Put them in a bucket and your toddler will be invested. Knowing your own toddler and their attention span, sometimes it's best to put two activities down so they can go back and forth for a while. That may help you get some good traction. You can find a tub to put these activities in at Lowe's. I got one for around $6.00, and it's a great size at twenty-four inches by thirty-six inches.

The point behind the activities is to plan ahead. Have these items stored ahead of time in Ziplock bags so you can easily grab your bucket and dump the activity right into it when you feel your toddler getting restless. It lets your child use their imagination to explore the items in the bin. There is no wrong way to play! Let your child do what they are going to do. I would have them work independently with these buckets or with another child. I would not guide them through this activity. Let them find their own inner voice that tells them what to do and how to do things. That way, it will be quick and painless for you because it will give you time to reboot, refocus, and reconnect with yourself.

## Transitions

Transitions between activities is another time that toddlers pick up on the unpredictability of what's coming up next. It's also important to have a great transition process in place because it helps toddlers predict when a fun activity will be coming to an end, which is hard for a toddler to understand. In order to continue to help them build their security skills, it is important to give them transition cues.

Any time a fun activity is coming to an end, it is important to give them notice. Start with a ten-minute notice. Set a timer, go over to your child, look him in the face and say, "Jake, in ten minutes, we have to clean up for lunch." After five minutes, repeat the process and say, "Jake, in five minutes, we have to clean up for lunch." When the timer goes off, start helping him clean up. This is not a negotiation. If this is a new transition process, he may cry, and that's fine. Cheerfully clean up and talk to him about how fun the activity was and what's coming up next. If he is having a tantrum, do not acknowledge it. Quickly move on to the next activity.

Do this transition process every time a transition activity occurs. He will begin to understand about how long he has left for an activity with a ten-minute warning, and he will begin to understand that having a tantrum will not affect the outcome of whether he gets to continue the activity or not. He will also begin to understand that the timer is responsible for the time, not Mommy, and that pleading with Mommy will not result in more time on the timer. Never add minutes to the timer. Anticipate the end of the activity, and be ready for the change when the timer goes off. A good transition system in place will cut down on a lot of tantrum behaviors.

## Logistical Planning

Planning ahead also involves places like the dreaded grocery store. How many times have you been the mom that has the child that screams for fun or screams because they want something you don't want them to have? We've all been there! It may seem obvious, but there are definite times when you *should not* go to the store. I would advise not going around nap time or mealtime.

I would also always slip a Ziplock bag of something in my purse. Have interesting snacks. Snacks they don't normally see at home. Anything out of the ordinary is exciting to a toddler. If you find yourself in a pinch, grab something off of the grocery store shelf and open as you walk through the aisles. The grocery store won't mind. Pay for it at the end. They would rather have a happy toddler than a screaming one! Believe me!

To make your trip painless and simple, I would also consider visualizing your expectation ahead of time. I would focus on it feeling good and you being happy. Nothing is more important than making sure that when you go to the grocery store, you're happy. Your toddler will reflect your attitude. If you're grouchy, your toddler will pay you right back.

Messes follow toddlers! You can never have too many baby wipes with you. Stick a bag of baby wipes in your purse. Check it often. They are multipurpose for all in the family, and they have saved us from a lot of emergencies. Just as a rule of thumb, in the car I always keep a back-up set of clothes, including socks and shoes. Extra diapers, extra wipes. In the winter, I keep an extra coat. Having these extras will save you time and money.

So, now that we have activity bags and shopping, let's plan ahead to start our day off right. We will talk about some internal environment planning in a later chapter, but for now, we are going to continue to talk about the external environment. I counted one day, when I stupidly left the dishwasher for unloading in the morning, how many times I got interrupted. I got interrupted *twelve times*! It took me one and a half hours to unload the dishwasher. During that time, I was called away to cook, to help someone on the potty, to break up a fight, to let the dog in, to get water, to make another waffle, to get a Band-Aid, to wipe a nose, and then I stopped counting.

I could've done it on my own the night before when everyone was asleep, in five minutes. Yes, I was tired, but it's days like this that make me tired. Days of poor planning, setting myself up for failure. Setting the babies up for failure and then being irritated when I have no one to blame but myself. Five short minutes could've saved me an hour and a half. I could've had three cups of coffee! Sitting down! Get the little stuff out of the way that your morning self will thank you for. I know you're tired, but it's so much harder to start your day behind.

Planning also involves any activities that involve going anywhere that isn't in the typical routine. If you're going to a park or the zoo, consider these questions. Is there anything you can do ahead of time that will save you the inconvenience at the location? Can you buy tickets online? Do they have bathrooms there? Will there be food? Should you pack food with you? What time period will you be there? Will the line from the zoo take you through the gift shop? How will your toddler handle that?

How can you prepare for that ahead of time? If you are vacationing with a toddler, call ahead to your accommodations and be aware of the set up. A hotel or VRBO should list everything on their website. Look at the family room layout. If you're spending a significant amount of time there, will you need a baby gate? Is there furniture you can maneuver once there to make room more accommodating for you? If the house has a pool, is it safe for a toddler or can a toddler easily access it?

If you are driving and will be spending a lot of time in the car, you will want to put together activity bags. Again, these should be cheap and easy, but something your toddler is not familiar with. You can also plan your drive to take short breaks in cities that have places like children's museums, so they can get out of the car, stretch, and crawl or walk around some. There are also a lot of iPad apps for toddlers.

Toddlers feel like mice a lot of the time. They never stay where you put them. It is in the planning of the details that makes it even feel possible. If you have to constantly parent from a place of "I'll be right back," or "Wait a minute," you will live a frustrating, interrupted life. Just a little bit of pre-planning gives you hours back during the week. Not only do you get hours back, but you get less of the constant monkey-on-your-back feeling that comes with parenting. Parenting is hard enough, but it is harder when you do it from a reactive position. This is a time in your life you'll never get back, and toddlers are wide open, soaking all of you in. Let them soak up who you really are and not the grouchy yeller you told yourself you were never going to be.

# 5

# BUILDING TRUST
# AND SECURITY

*"If you talk about it, it's a dream, if you envision
it, it's possible, but if you schedule it, it's real"*
*-Tony Robbins*

I had been watching a nest of baby robins for weeks. I watched
the blue eggs magically turn into babies, and I watched the
mama bird reliably and capably return each day to feed them.
They grew and got more rambunctious, and mama bird would
always return with more food to a nest of open mouths. One
day, I was alerted to mama robin almost screeching. Because
the noise was alarming and I feared danger for her babies, I
went to check her nest. Mama bird sat on a fence post nearby,
willing each baby robin to try their new wings for flight. She
knew they were strong enough, and her confidence in their
ability empowered each tiny bird to take its first flight from
the safety of the nest to the fence post beside her. I was in awe
to see such a moment among a mama of nature and her babies
and was hopeful that I, too, was inspiring the same confidence
in my own children, that when they were ready to fly, their

wings would be strong enough to carry them through each season of life.

As soon as possible, we want to train our children to understand autonomy and foster in them a deep sense of security, so that when they try their own wings for the first time, they are fail-proof. It's hard to know how to set your child up successfully while still trying to shelter them from the ugliness that remains in the world. We can only show them how to read the roadmap of life and how to use their compass to guide them, so if they lose their way, they can always find their way back to the nest.

Learning how to read the roadmap of life comes early and when done well, the lessons are frequent and effective. However, there are building blocks that each child must develop in order to be an effective roadmap reader. The first is a sense of security. A child must gain a sense of security for physical and emotional development. It is crucial to building relationships with others. Security also determines how a child feels about themselves and their environment. How secure a child feels is an easy predictor of future success. Security also allows a child to trust themselves. One way in which a child learns to feel secure in their environment is through a consistency in your mood, and in what you say and follow through on. Your child is learning about how their needs are met, but they are also learning how to interact with others, their environment, and themselves.

## Follow-Through and Consistency

I have two brothers and two sisters. My children are eleven and nine, but between my siblings, there are six children aged three or younger, with one more on the way. It's like toddler heaven, and I just get to watch! For our most recent vacation, we went to a beautiful lake. It was lovely, but extremely inconvenient for my four siblings with small children. First, it was on the steepest hill I've ever seen. There was no outside area for children, except for a gravel fire pit and a two-story dock, with a slide! For my children, it was magical; they could jump and swim all day. For my siblings, it was touch and go at every moment. When they weren't keeping their children from drowning outside, they were keeping their children safe from Jake, inside.

Jake is a very smart three-year-old who lacks volume control. He's as feisty as he is sweet. When he doesn't have your attention, he'll throw a stack of plastic cups in the air to make sure you know he's around. Jake has given up naps, so it's hard to get him through a whole day of vacation activity on one night of rest. By the end of the day, he is running on fumes.

His behavior, at that point, was emotional. He was either laughing or crying, all at the highest volume. A parent had stepped in to help him negotiate with his cousin, who is also three, and who may already be a master negotiator. Whatever was being told to Jake, was not what he wanted to hear and he continued to get more upset, which escalated his parent. His well-meaning and lovely parent would always respond with, "Do you want to go home?" "Do you want to go to bed?" "I'm taking you downstairs," "You're going to go to bed now," all in hopes of de-escalating the situation. The problem in a situation like that is young children cannot rationalize. He was not motivated by negative consequences, and there was no follow through on any of the de-escalation tactics regardless. So, the take away for Jake was, "When I don't like something, I scream and a parent comes to help me. I can't really hear what my parent is telling me because I'm too busy being irrational."

If you are at the point where your toddler is over emotional, over tired, over stimulated, it is not time to ask him what he would like. It is time to decide for him. Remove him from the overstimulating environment, so he can calm down. Do not ask him if he'd like to go. He will never agree. Pick him up and go. Take him on a walk, take him to a quiet room, take him on a car ride, look for things that are yellow, or blue, or green, search for squares. Anything that can stop the overstimulation and reset his brain. Once he is calm, you can reassess what he really needs. Why is he acting this way? Is he tired? Is he hungry? Is he bored? Then, once you know what the problem is, solve his problem.

Remember the birds flying to the mom on the fence at the beginning of the chapter? The birds flew to the mom because they trusted her. Another important step to teaching your child how to read their roadmap in life is building trust. A toddler learns to trust their outer world and inner world based on their caregiver's follow-through, from birth. Did their caregiver pick them up when they cried, were they fed when they were hungry? Were the basic needs of the child met? As the toddler ages, this trust is put into words. When you say, "Clean up time is in ten minutes," and you demonstrate that consistently, the child learns to rely on the fact that the outside world is trustworthy. This builds independence. As they start to trust, they can maneuver the outside world somewhat on their own. A child's emotional security is tied to the emotional response of their caregiver. If the caregiver was constantly angered by the baby or toddler, the child is less trusting of their environment and of themselves.

Trust and security are crucial pieces for mood and stability as children develop. If their environment is unpredictable, and the people in their environment are unreliable, the child's emotional needs are not being met. It is harder for a child to learn coping skills and how to manage emotions if they do not have appropriate guidance. They will also never learn to trust their own instincts when they can't rely on their caregivers.

## Setting Limits

Follow-through helps children develop healthy boundaries. Children *should* test the limits. It's a natural progression as they learn to use their independence skills. Testing the limits, however, can't start unless they have clear limits to begin with. If they live a life without a limitation from the beginning, then the development of their own self suffers. They are too busy trying to navigate the unsafe world of chaos. Make limits easy for young children to understand. Make sure limits are consistent among parents. For example, if eating at the table is important to you, both parents have to be willing to reinforce the limit. Lastly, and most importantly, when setting limits ask yourself, "Why is this a limit?" If it is for safety, then the answer is clear. If you are limiting a child because an activity is messy or loud, remember that a child's job is play! A child must also be allowed to follow their own bliss. If their life is extremely limited, the natural progression of learning how to use their own emotional guidance system suffers. Children then learn that it is only important to please their caregiver, when the real job of the caregiver is to teach the child how to live a life of happiness.

## Establishing a Routine

Jane, my fiery redhead who I watch during the day, had been home with her mama all morning. When she dropped Jane off at lunchtime, Jane instantly ran over to her highchair and pulled it out to be set up. Her mom looked at me perplexed and said, "We haven't been able to get her to sit in a high chair for months."

I thought about it for a second and responded, "Well, she wants to eat." I wasn't being sarcastic, just honest. It wasn't a choice at my house. At times, I had up to five babies. If they wanted to eat, they were all going to be properly contained. Logistically, it wouldn't have worked any other way. That conversation came up in my mind often over the years. Jane sat in the highchair because that is where her food was served. When she was finished, she got out. Of course over the years, she asked to get out before she was finished, but the consequence of that was that food did not go with her. I was not a negotiator. I wouldn't even discuss food. The only thing I ever asked her if she told me she was hungry was if she wanted to get back into her highchair. If she had decided to cry or carry on about it, I would not acknowledge it. The acknowledgement alone invites the negotiation tomorrow, and tomorrow the food will still be served in the high chair.

Part of sticking to a routine for a child is being routine inside of the routine. In the above example about the high chair, at my house, food was served in the high chair because of convenience. You have to be clear about your desire while establishing a routine. If you let your child snack on crackers while doing an activity in the living room one day, and you want him to sit in the high chair the next day, expect a tantrum! If you want consistent behavior, do not have wishy-washy expectations. Sleeping times and eating times are a tantrum-prone time because your child is already tired or hungry. This is not the time to try something new or to give your child unpredictability.

Routines make life predictable for young children. Predictable patterns make children feel more in control of their environment. Behaviors such as tantrums often show up when children are feeling out of control. Generally, toddlers are taking one longer afternoon nap. Below is a sample schedule I used for toddlers. My toddlers could do this schedule without me present, that's how predictable it was for them. It was like they were on autopilot. It made life so much easier because we weren't constantly re-negotiating our plan. I would give them one-word reminders about what was coming up and then I would give them the ten-minute timer. If lunch was coming up I would say, "Ten minutes, clean up and hands." They would know it's time to clean up and after cleanup, we were washing our hands. When the timer went off I would say, "Hands and lunch." They would have a reminder to wash their hands, then they would know to go to the lunch table. Limiting your words allows toddlers to draw a quick focus, they don't have time to tune you out, and it's easy for them to remember.

## Sample Schedule

7:30 AM      breakfast

7:45-9:30      AM-morning activities: you can either use the table bucket activities from previous chapter or let the child play by themselves

| | |
|---|---|
| 9:30-9:45 | AM-snack |
| 9:45-11:00 | AM-potty, then outside time or an out of house activity |
| 11:00 AM | wash hands and lunch |
| 11:30 AM | books or table activities, e.g. playdough, potty |
| 12:00 PM | nap. Keep them in their crib as long as possible. If they are climbing out, you can buy an over the crib net on Amazon. When you take them out of the crib, your life will never be the same! |
| 2:30 PM | wake up, potty, snack |
| 3:00 PM | afternoon activities, either table bucket activities from previous chapter or let child play by themselves |
| 4:45 PM | potty, then outside walk if it's nice |
| 5:30 PM | electronic time while you get dinner ready |
| 6:00 PM | wash hands and dinner |
| 6:30 PM | potty and bath |
| 7:00 PM | books and playing |
| 7:30 PM | potty and bed |

Find a schedule that works best for you and your child. The key here is consistency and predictability. It allows them to feel some control over their environment by being able to predict what comes next. There is no wrong way to do a schedule, or wrong time to do an activity. Do what feels right for you.

## Sleep

> *"You don't 'fix' your child. You create conditions for them to rise"*
>
> -Dr. Shefali Tsabary

Sleep is a big concern for most parents. "Does my child sleep enough?" "Why can't I get my child to sleep?" "How do I develop a good bedtime routine?" Every child is different, so the amount of sleep each child needs is also different. You need to find the magic number for your child. The Center for Disease Control suggests that children one to two years of age should sleep somewhere between eleven to fourteen hours a day, while children three to five years of age should sleep somewhere between ten to thirteen hours a day.

Sleep deprivation isn't always obvious in a toddler. Often times, toddlers become more active when they haven't had enough sleep. Lack of sleep makes it harder for them to concentrate and they become over-excited and restless. They have a harder time falling asleep. Toddlers with too little sleep may be grouchy or irritable or more emotional than usual. They may fall asleep while playing on the floor outside of their normal sleeping hours. If you find that your toddler's behavior is consistent with the symptoms of sleep deprivation, try putting him to sleep earlier. It may have seemed because he wasn't falling asleep easily and was more active than usual that he was getting too much sleep when in actuality, he needs more sleep. If you feel like your toddler is getting too much sleep and their nighttime sleep is becoming affected, decrease the amount of time they sleep during the day. If your toddler typically takes a two-hour nap, have them take a one-hour nap and see if that improves their nighttime sleep.

In order to establish an easy bedtime routine, consistency is key. Pick an evening schedule that can be easily followed by your family, and follow it every evening. A good example of a bedtime routine is as follows:

- Dinner
- Bath
- Read book
- Connect with your child over the day, discuss what you are grateful for
- Set the transition timer for ten minutes
  o During the timer, brush teeth, go potty
- When timer goes off, child goes in crib. Do not linger, cheerfully say good-night and leave room

It is important to remember as you transition into the beginning of the bedtime routine that you do not engage in activity that is overstimulating. This includes developing boundaries when it comes to electronics. If electronics become part of your daily schedule, do not incorporate them at bedtime. Electronics are overstimulating and are also an activity that most toddlers love, and tempting your toddler with a tantrum at bedtime is not a good idea. Even if you are on vacation or you spent half of the day doing something other than your normal routine, it is important to get back on the routine as soon as possible. There is nothing worse than a grouchy toddler at the beach. You can minimize his negative behavior by giving him predictable outcomes.

Building trust and security with your child encompasses a lot of aspects. Nothing is more important than being consistent and following through. Your child comes to rely on your stability as a symbol for the stability of how they view the world. Being able to establish clear limits while still allowing your child to maintain a fun, playful environment, and creating a routine to provide predictability and structure will greatly reduce your toddler's tantrums.

## Part 2

# PREPARING YOUR INTERNAL ENVIRONMENT

# 6

## POWER IN THE PRESENT

*"Drink your tea slowly and reverently, as if it is
the axis on which the world earth revolves-slowly,
evenly, without rushing toward the future. Live
the actual moment. Only this moment is life"*
-Thich Nhat Hanhs

### Conscious Living

Now that you have focused on the activities and structure in the environment for your toddler, and you are faithfully following a routine and are consistent with your follow-through, you should be noticing big improvements. You should be feeling more in control and ready to shift some of your focus inward. This is where real sustaining life changes can happen in any aspect of your life.

Learning how to live presently has been the biggest gift to myself. Back in the deepest days of my depression, I went to counseling; in fact, over the years, I have tried several counselors. I would start each session the same way. "I need coping skills so when my anxiety gets out of hand, I know what to do." I had already tried Xanax and other benzodiazepines, which did take away the anxiety, but they made my body slow, my judgement clouded, and took away any sort of clarity, which is obviously important in day-to-day living. I found anxiety so debilitating, I would've shaved my head or walked places backwards if someone told me that's what worked. Each counseling session went about the same way: we would talk about a past event, how it made me feel, why I felt that way, but there was never an actionable idea to solve the problem. Counselor after counselor, it seemed to go the same way and, for me, the outcome was of no benefit. Talking about the problem, or events that led to the problem, never fixed the problem for me. Therapy made me feel tired and emotional.

I never necessarily understood what being "present "meant. I was always around, so how could I not be present? The more I started to identify with the word "present," and define it for myself, the more I understood that I actually was never present. If I could relate it to where I actually was spending my mental time, you could say my thoughts constantly brought me to the past. Past issues I had, past situations I could've handled better, past scenarios I would've played out differently. Or, you could say, I was living future. Future daydreams, what if scenarios, playing them out in my mind, usually worst- case-scenario type situations. If my future actually showed up like I was imagining, in end to end worst-case scenario situations, I would've been dead years ago.

It wasn't until I actively started considering what my thoughts did for me that I begin to understand I actually never really lived in the present. Being present is another way of saying conscious, or aware. It's actually living without thought from the past or without thought about the future. It's actually living in the now. If you consider now, it is the only thing that ever exists. You only actually ever live in the unending present. It never changes to the future and it never goes back to the past. Something magical starts to happen when you live in the present. It doesn't sound complicated, but when you really start to think about your life, how often are you really present? The only way to live the future of your dreams is to find bliss in the present. When you fundamentally realize the only important moment is now you will begin to live differently. When you realize the future of your dreams relies on living a happier and happier present, you will focus on the present. You will see that the past does not allow you to live a happier and happier present, so it seems pointless to relive it over and over. When you truly understand the importance of present living you will feel a shift about how you feel about the past and the future. They will become far less important.

Sitting with one of my two-year olds one morning, I wanted to consciously participate in the activity with him. I wanted to release any thoughts about the past, and I didn't want to think about the future, I just wanted to remain present in the activity with him. Even though we were only shape patterning, the activity was liberating. I felt free from the bondage that held me every day, reliving past failures. I thought the only way I could improve as a person was to sit in the shame and guilt of my past and suffer. It also freed me from the worst-case-scenario future events that I felt doomed to live because of my past failures. In actuality, the failures that I made up for myself were far more severe than any actual event. It's part of our ego's way of saying we aren't good enough, we could've done better. Sitting in the present moment begins to make you wonder, "What was I hoping to solve by reliving it over and over?"

I felt a little silly having such an "a-ha" moment doing shape patterns with a two-year-old. I felt more creative flow and ideas when I was actively being present than when I was actually trying to be creative by reliving creative experiences in the past.

When remaining present with your toddler, it can really affect their behavior. Anytime you are distracted by thoughts, devices, or TV, your toddler can pick up on that. A toddler only understands that he is the center of the world. He doesn't understand that you actually have other things to do. For example, you're out for a walk, and he notices a squirrel in a tree. He has had to try to get your attention three times, but you are distracted looking at your phone. He gets escalated, and you are not noticing because you are still distracted. That escalation's going to build momentum throughout the rest of the morning if you are constantly distracted. As a busy mother, certainly you have things to do. When engaging with your toddler, keep in mind there are activities that you can do for yourself that can keep you present, and there are activities that should be saved for when he's either sleeping or engaged in an activity of his own.

## Mindful Activities

If you have a hard time staying present, there are some ideas to keep you mindful. Mindful is just being aware of where your thoughts are. Some quick and easy mindful activities are becoming aware of your breathing. Stop what you're doing, set a timer for two minutes, and for that two minutes, just focus on breathing in and breathing out each breath for ten seconds. This activity helps stop momentum on thoughts that are already active within you.

Another great mindful activity is to stop what you're doing and focus on finding five birds outside. Notice the color of the birds, what breed they are, if they're making noise or if they're flying or if they're sitting in a tree. Notice how when you start to look around in your environment, it stops unwanted thoughts. These are good activities to try with your toddler as well. Some great mindful activities for him maybe looking around the room and looking for something yellow. You may ask him to see if he can spot three circles. He cannot continue a tantrum and do this activity at the same time. It uses two separate parts of the brain.

Another mindful activity for your toddler may be whispering something silly in his ear. Whisper it so he cannot hear it, and he will ask you to repeat it. Continue to whisper silly things in his ear throughout the day. Doing these mindful activities together will help him focus his attention quickly on the present. It will also be a good reminder for you to stop living in the past and to start living in the now present.

Anytime you see your toddler start to escalate, you can quickly pop in a mindful activity. This will stop his negative momentum quickly, and the easiest time to stop a tantrum is right when it is beginning to start.

## Discipline vs Conscious Parenting?

As a mother and someone in the field of child development, the question of discipline is always in my mind. My philosophies of discipline, like most things in my life, have changed as I have become aware of how energy is in the world. I intention-ally went away from discipline and more towards conscious parenting. I am going to define discipline and conscious parenting as I understand them to be.

I understand discipline as imposing a negative consequence on someone for a negative behavior. I understand conscious parenting to be intentionally deciding to let my child follow their own guidance system if it does not affect their safety, even if it makes me uncomfortable.

Let's talk about some examples. First, let me start by saying conscious parenting is not a free for all! Quite the opposite. It is about staying present with your child and, as negative behaviors show up, stopping them before they get momentum.

## Example

Jake is a feisty three-year-old with a giant sense of adventure. He is extremely smart. He knows all of his letters and numbers, he can speak in full sentences. He is on vacation with all of his aunts and uncles, grandparents, and several of his cousins that are around his age or younger. One of his cousins, Scarlett, who is also three and extremely smart and can speak in full sentences, likes to play more by herself.

## Scenario

Jake wants to play with Scarlett. He wants to play Rapunzel. She insists that there can only be one of them named Rapunzel, and she is going to be Rapunzel. This irritates Jake, and he starts to get loud and yell at Scarlett.

## Discipline

Parent intervenes because they don't want it to keep escalating. Parent tries to rationalize with Jake about how Scarlett is feeling. This continues to upset Jake who is now screaming and crying. He kicks at Scarlett. Parent grabs Jake and tells him to say sorry to Scarlett. Jake refuses. Jake has to go downstairs for a time out. Jake returns after about fifteen minutes with dad. Jake is not crying but he's still complaining that he wants to be Rapunzel.

## Conscious Parenting

Realizing there is split energy all over the room, parenting is working hard on keeping frequency at a high, stable level. Parent realizes that anything other than ease and flow is flowing into the experience because her vibration is allowing it. As soon as parent hears the word Rapunzel, she steps in next to Jake. Parent knows how important Rapunzel is to Jake. Parent gets excited about the kids playing Rapunzel and suggests that this special occasion Rapunzel has a twin brother, also named Rapunzel. This makes Jake and Scarlett both giggle. They agree and continue playing without incident.

In the discipline scenario, the negative behavior continued to get attention which caused it to get momentum. When energy has momentum in a positive or negative direction, it is harder to stop. If a child is in a negative momentum, they also cannot access their infinite intelligence, which is their guidance system. When children are tapped into their guidance system, they will always make decisions inspired to them. In the conscious parenting example, the child never left their positive vibration. Therefore, the positive behavior continued to get momentum.

# Kindness

*"Being kind isn't always easy. Or convenient. But it has the potential to change everything."*

*-hplyrikz.com*

My three-year-old friend, Jane, has beautiful, long, bright red hair. Whenever we go anywhere, people comment on it. Although she is not my daughter, I have stopped trying to explain that and just started accepting the compliments. My hair, on the other hand, has always had a growth "stopping" point. I'm jealous of Jane's beautiful thick red hair. One day, tired of my own, thin, dried out hair, I cut it off where it was clearly breaking off, but it was a noticeable six inches. It was late in the afternoon and I was in view of the babies in the baby room so I could keep an eye on them as they played. I cut off my hair, blew it dry and styled it. Everyone that came in my home that afternoon mentioned that my haircut was cute, and I would say how I had done it myself, and then we would all giggle about what a terrible idea that was.

That weekend, I received a text message from Jane's mom with a picture. Jane too, had decided she needed a haircut! She had gotten the scissors and carefully cut several uneven inches out of her beautiful, long, baby red hair. I was mortified! I knew exactly what had happened. She saw me cut my hair so she decided it was a good idea to cut her hair.

Children are always watching their caregivers. That's where they pick up all of their clues on how to manage themselves in the world. I didn't explain to Jane what I was doing, I didn't even talk to her about it. However, she modeled my behavior exactly. Your children are always watching you.

Now that you can slow the negative thoughts, and you are becoming aware of what you are thinking, it's important to choose your thoughts with purpose. Kindness has far reaching benefits in your life:

- Kindness allows your children to view the world with a more optimistic view when they have kind parents.
- Kind parents have kinder children.
- It can reduce stress and anxiety when you are kind to others.
- Kindness releases feel good hormones in your body.
- Kindness is good for your heart.
- Kindness reduces illness.

According to David R. Hamilton, in his book *Why Kindness is Good For You*, when we are kind it changes the way we view ourselves and the world. We see ourselves as more compassionate and useful and feel less guilt and shame in our lives. We give people in our lives the benefit of the doubt. We are more helpful and get involved in altruistic activities such as volunteering.

Other helpful ideas to build thinking in a positive direction.

- Gratitude – write down in a journal everything you are grateful for. Do this frequently.
- At bedtime, list with your children things you are grateful for.
- Forgiveness – write a letter to a person you are trying to forgive, even if you don't send it.
- Forgiveness is letting the hold someone has over you go and realizing you have the ability to feel good regardless.
- Exercise – participate in physical activities.

- Appreciation – make a habit of walking around and actively listing things you see that you appreciate.

Build a network of support around yourself of like-minded people. Stay away from others who build negative momentum. Surrounding yourself with kind, happy people will ensure that you will stay kind and happy!

# 7

## GOING WITHIN

*"Holding onto anger is like drinking poison*
*and expecting the other person to die"*
*-Buddha*

## Meditation

I was pretty sure that meditation existed for *everyone but* me. Buddhist monks, new age people in California, cute yoga girls in skinny outfits drinking fancy coffee, for sure, but not me. I would feel silly or stupid. I wasn't even sure the point of meditation. I could pretend to relax in my bed at night. What was the difference?

I had gotten to a point in my depression that I was scared. I was afraid I would never be able to discern a happy feeling again. I remember sitting in my "baby" room, on the floor, thinking, "Am I ever going to feel better?" Willing myself to feel anything. Getting up, moving my body, watching Tony Robbins on YouTube, yelling like an idiot when he said yell to shift my energy. I was scared. I was at the bottom, and I didn't know how to get out. I was actively seeing a doctor for depression, taking medication, but I needed to do something different. It was that day, whatever that day was, that I started to take my own life back.

I started slowly with meditation. After all, I still wasn't sure of the point, but once I start something I am usually "all in." I did research on the internet and just picked guided meditations on YouTube that I liked. I didn't know what I was after. Often times throughout the entire meditation, the little person in my brain would talk to me the entire time. I would do everything I could to shut it up. They suggested sending thoughts out on clouds, which I did...then I thought about watching the clouds drift away with my thoughts. I will tell you it is not easy to quiet your mind that has a lot of momentum of thought in the wrong direction. It takes practice. I will promise you though, after a few days' time, I started to notice a difference. I could quiet my mind for a couple of minutes here and there during meditations, and when the momentum of the negative thoughts stopped, I could feel relief.

I promised myself I would meditate every day for the first thirty days because I had read about the enormous benefit to help with depression. I had no idea the enormous benefit it was going to have on my entire life. I have learned how to have self-love and appreciation, and I have found happiness and peace.

## Where to Start?

The great part about meditation is that you're not going to do it wrong. You don't have to watch a "how to meditate" video in order to do it correctly. The entire goal of meditation is to quiet your mind. In the beginning or on particularly hectic days, maybe you can only clear your mind for two minutes in a twenty-minute meditation. That's enough. It is the runaway negative thoughts that create all of your problems, and those are the thoughts we are stopping.

You can choose to lay down or sit up. Find a quiet place where you can have uninterrupted time. The morning is best, because it will set your day on the right path, but choose any time of day that works best for you. Take slow deep breaths and focus on your breathing. Every time a thought pops in your head, which may be nonstop at the beginning of a meditation, envision the thought on a cloud in your mind and let it float away. What helps me the most when I have a lot of thoughts is picturing a tiny woman in my head producing the thoughts. I just lay her down and envision her sleeping.

Bring your awareness back to your breathing. You may feel tingling in your body, this is just energy movement and is normal. Continue this process for the desired amount of time. There are many, many guided meditations on YouTube which can help with focus because they give you something to "think" about. You should have a feeling of detachment after you get the hang of meditating. You should come out of meditation feeling more mentally clear, emotionally calm, and stable.

Consider every topic you've ever thought about as having a little up or down switch in your brain. When the switch is up, it means the wanted benefits are showing up in your life. Let's assume the switch is water. Assume you have as much water as you want in your life because your switch for water, is turned up. It could be turned up for multiple reasons. One, because you believe water is plentiful. Two, because you think water is easy to get. If your water switch was turned off in your brain, water would not be showing up in your life. It could be for several reasons. It could be because you thought water was scarce or because water was expensive. Meditation helps you reset your switches. As you start to feel better and better you will start to see that your switches are just preprogrammed by your subconscious and reality is a collection of old thoughts that can be changed. Anything in your reality is a manifested old thought. It manifested because it had momentum. If you don't like something in your reality, you have to change your thoughts and feelings about it. Meditation will stop the momentum of all thought and allow you to think from a more neutral position.

## Benefits of Meditation

Mental health is an epidemic in the United States. According to the Center for Disease Control, fifty percent of all Americans will be diagnosed with a mental illness at some point in their lifetime. Mental illnesses such as depression are the third most common cause of hospitalization in the United States for those aged eighteen to forty-four, and adults living with serious mental illness die on an average of twenty-five years earlier than others. There are scientifically proven benefits to meditation:

- Reduces Stress – A study in the National Institute of Health included 3,500 adults, whose inflammation response to the stress hormone of cortisol decreased after eight weeks of mindfulness meditation. Many studies have been done on whether mediation helps stress, and it appears it not only helps stress, but also stress related conditions such as fibromyalgia, PTSD, and irritable bowel syndrome.

57

- Reduces Anxiety – A study published in PsycNET found that mindfulness meditation helped health care workers with on-the-job stress, which was leading to increased depression and low job satisfaction.
- Promotes Emotional Health – The National Institute of Health published a study which showed decreased depression in 4600 adults in two studies.
- Enhances Self-Awareness – meditation helps you develop a stronger sense of self and how you relate to others. Forty men and women in their senior years took part in a meditation trial as part of a study, and their loneliness decreased in comparison to those on the waiting list for the study.
- Helps increase attention span and decrease age related memory loss – The National Institute of Health has several studies published on the benefits of memory and how it relates to meditation.
- May help generate kindness – In the practice of metta-meditation or loving kindness meditation, one study show that positive feelings developed in the meditation can improve social anxiety, reduce marriage conflict, and help with anger management.
- May help fight addiction – The National Institute of Health has published studies based on food, alcohol, and drug addiction and found that meditation has helped with will power, craving control, and reduced stress.
- Improves sleep – meditation helps slow the momentum of thoughts to help with insomnia.
- Helps control pain – several studies have been done to show the effectiveness of meditation to help control pain.

Brain scans have been done on meditators and non-meditators when exposed to a pain stimulus, and those who meditate showed increased activity in the area of the brain that controls pain. In a larger study of 3500 participants, it showed that meditators had decreased complaints of chronic or intermittent pain.

- Can decrease blood pressure – an article published in the National Institute of Health showed 996 participants meditated on a silent mantra, and their blood pressure dropped an average of five points.

With all of these proven benefits, we do a poor job teaching our children how to take care of their emotional bodies. There are also some great choices of mindful meditation for children. YouTube has guided meditations that are stories, which allow them to follow along and still gain the meditation benefits. Below is a list of different types of meditation, some of which will help both you and your children. Meditation, when done regularly, just becomes a regular part of the day, like brushing your teeth. We all live in a fast-paced world, but clearly, with fifty percent of our society having a mental health illness, we are not coping well. Children need to be able to un-trigger their fight or flight response once it is turned on. Our human bodies are not capable of withstanding years of being bombarded with stress hormones from stress we are not managing well. Any of these types of meditations will bring the practitioner out of a negative pattern of thinking and back to the present moment.

# Types of Meditation

There are several types of meditation and within each type, there are different categories. Try not to get intimidated; there is no wrong way to do it, and the entire point is to detach and clear your mind. The more often you do it, the more comfortable you will get. Here are some of the more popular types of meditation.

## Loving-Kindness Meditation-Metta

This meditation focuses on sending love towards everything, including enemies and sources of stress. The practitioner opens themselves up to receive love and kindness, while sending out messages of love and kindness. They repeat this process until they feel love and kindness. Helps those who struggle with anger, conflict, rage, and interpersonal relationships. Reduces depression, stress, and stress related conditions.

## Body Scan or Progressive Relaxation

The practitioner scans their body for tension during this meditation and once found, focuses until release. They start at one end of the body and move to the other end. Sometimes a visualization technique is used to release tension, and sometimes tensing of all muscles is performed and then released. Helps promote calmness, relaxation, and has also been known to help with chronic pain. Can help with insomnia.

## Mindfulness

The practitioner can do this almost anywhere. Mindfulness reminds practitioners to remain present and aware in the moment. This can be done in a line at a grocery store. Practitioner stays present and focused without thinking future or past thoughts and does not have judgement about the situation. Here, the practitioner is the observer. Helps reduce negative emotions and negative reactions. Improves overall well-being.

## Breath Awareness

Practitioner focuses only on patterned breath. Practitioner ignores all other thoughts that enter the mind. This is a form of mindfulness meditation and has similar health benefits.

## Kundalini Yoga

Physical form of meditation. Practitioner learns poses and breathwork during mediation while performing mantras. Energy centers are activated in chakras located by spine and above head. Helps reduce pain. Can improve mental health by reducing anxiety and depression.

## Zen

Form of meditation, usually part of a Buddhist practice. Practitioners study under a teacher because of the specific steps and postures involved. Focus on breathing, becoming aware of one thought without judgement. Similar to mindfulness, but requires more discipline. Often includes a spiritual path.

## Transcendental

Spiritual form where practitioner sits in seated posture. Goal of this meditation is to rise out of physical body. Focus on mantras. Complex mantras are used. Usually a teacher guides the practitioner.

Children need to see and be able to model healthy and quick ways to handle stress. Toddlers love practicing mindfulness and meditation, and it is never to early to start, even if it's just two minutes a day!

# 8

## CALMING YOUR INNER WORLD

*"In the same way that a magnet is attracted
to steel, we draw into our lives energy that
resonates at a similar frequency to our own"*
*-Christy Whitman*

I had an "awakening" on December 1, 2018. That's when my life changed forever. First off, I didn't even know what an awakening was. An awakening is considered coming into awareness about the "aware" part of you. You have five sense perceptions that give you information about the environment or an experience. Then, there is part of you that is "aware" of the perception and of the experience. That awareness is what people refer to as a soul, or God-source. It has changed every part of my life, mostly with children and how I parent.

I have a degree in early childhood education, I have worked with toddlers for decades. My mom had toddlers when I was a teenager, and I was constantly helping. I babysat all through high school and college. I had my own kids. I worked at a child development center as a teacher and a director, and I had my own in-home daycare for years. But, everything about children has changed for me since my awakening experience. It is a bit complicated, and I wouldn't go through the entire process if I didn't think you too could benefit. I want to let you know that you are the only one in control. I want you to be able to stand in your power and understand what is really happening with your toddler. Every time something in your experience goes a bit sideways, you should stop and ask yourself, "What is going on with me?"

## Universal Law of Attraction and Vibration

First, everything on this Earth is made of energy – tables, chairs, people, everything. If you had a microscope and looked through it at a chair, you would see that the particles inside of the chair are vibrating. That vibration gives off a frequency, like a radio station. The chair has a different frequency than a human, and different humans have different frequencies. We jump around all over the place. I know this seems insane to read about in a book about toddler tantrums, except that it has *everything* to do with toddler tantrums, so bear with me.

This Universe is a law-based Universe, and it operates with different laws, like the Law of Gravity. You don't have to know about gravity to "use" it, it just automatically works for you. The Law of Attraction (LOA) is the same way. You don't have to know about it in order for it to work for you, but it is always working for you regardless. The Law of Attraction states that like attracts like, meaning it draws similar energies together.

Thoughts and feelings have a frequency, like a radio wave. You can't see a radio wave, but from past experiences, you know they exist. It's the same concept as a dog whistle. You cannot hear a dog whistle for yourself, but because of the dog's reaction, you perceive that an energy went into the air and was heard or felt by the dog. This is the same with thoughts and feelings. Every thought or feeling goes out as energy and attracts like thoughts and feelings. That is why your thoughts gain momentum, and it is harder to stop thoughts after you have been thinking them awhile. When a negative thought goes out, it attracts a thought on the same frequency. Put enough thoughts together, and those thoughts form emotions. Emotions are even more powerful attractors. Thoughts are electric and emotions are magnetic. There is an electromagnetic field that can be measured around the human body. Once you start feeling at a frequency, your personal reality starts to take place in that frequency. Let's say you're feeling hopeless. When you go out into the world, the Universe will provide you examples of hopelessness, and your energy will pull you toward other people on that same frequency.

You have the opportunity in every moment to make a quantum shift to a different frequency. You can tell which frequency your shifting to by the emotion you feel. The better you feel, the higher the frequency. Each time you shift the future changes based on which frequency you jumped to. That is why living in the present moment is so important. It is only in the present moment that you can make the conscious choice to feel good. When you think about the past, you are feeling the same emotions. Those emotions tell you what frequency you are on. When you think about the past, you are creating more past for your future! If you want a different future, you have to create the feelings that you want to feel in your future in order to tune into that frequency. Applying this to your practical situation, you want your toddler to stop having a tantrums. What does a future free from tantrums feel like? What would it feel like being in control of your life? What would it feel like being the mother I want to be? Spend more time feeling the feelings you want in your future than the feelings you have from your past.

Look around your life now. Everything in it, every single thing and experience, good and bad, you have attracted. It doesn't mean, for example, if you've had a broken bone, you literally asked for a broken bone. But, it means maybe you held on to fear, and that fear got momentum. That momentum became emotion, and that emotion manifested in your body. This is just an example of how the Universe works.

The same goes for things. Do a small experiment with yourself. Start to think of something that isn't important to you, but give it some momentum. Think of it for thirty seconds. For example, start to think about a red balloon. What would it feel like? What would it smell like? What shape would it be? How would you feel if you saw it? Spend a couple of minutes visualizing red balloons. After a few minutes, release the thought. Do not attach to the outcome, just go on about your normal day. When you start to see red balloons, acknowledge that you are seeing them, just to yourself, and you will start to see more. Feel feelings of appreciation for the balloons. It works every time for anything. I like to know when I am in a state when my thoughts can manifest easily. I think about Range Rovers a lot. I know when I start to see a lot of Range Rovers, I'm letting my thoughts flow without resistance. I do this experiment every day. Some days I can see up to thirty Range Rovers driving around!

Now, in the Law of Attraction, the Universe is a cooperative component, and it is drawing like frequencies together. This is where it really gets interesting and life changing! Everything you witness in your experience will be an exact match to your vibration. There is no assertion, only attraction. It would be impossible for anything that is not a match to your vibration to come into your experience. However, your attention to unwanted or unpleasant situations can lower your vibration and allow the situation into your experience. Whatever is happening in your experience will make you aware of your point of attraction. We are literally shaping our own reality. That's why you're drawn to certain people and repelled by others.

When you are able to raise your frequency, intuition becomes clearer. You will be inspired and drawn to do certain things. It is your own energy pulling you because you have a better, closer tap on Source energy. The thoughts you receive are from the highest frequency version of yourself. The self that knows you are limitless and boundless and is calling to you through your intuition and emotional resources. However, you can only hear what that version of you is saying when you are feeling good enough to be at a high enough frequency. So, I've told you thoughts become things and you wonder how that's possible because you've thought about a lot of things you would like and they haven't shown up. All of those wonderful things that could improve your life are in a high frequency vibration. Every single thought about any experience you've had and the improvement of it is living with you in and your highest frequency self. While your awareness is on this frequency. *Change your awareness!* In each moment of your life choose something that feels better and think about it and keep making tiny quantum leaps. Your life will get better and better and better. How fast you make the jump is up to you and your ability to remain in a frequency unconditionally, even when conditions around you attempt to pull you from it.

Children are pure Source energy. They are wide open sponges until they are around seven, and are happy to feed right into your vibrational atmosphere. Right now there is a lot of momentum around the idea of your child having tantrums. Your thoughts need to change to "my child is happy." If you continue to think that your child will have tantrums, they will have tantrums. It is your continued attention to their behavior that creates more tantrums. Most of the time, they are just following their bliss, and you decide that a rule is more important. It may be that you want them to stay neat and tidy, or that you want the house to stay clean, or that you want them to do something quieter, or that you are frustrated because he is making too much noise for other people. If he is happy, let him be happy. Either way, you tend to your vibrational atmosphere, and pretty soon, it won't be hard to have a good time with your toddler. It will be fun to go out. It is fun to be happy. It is easier to be happy. Life is easier when you are happy. You can be anyone you want. Choose happy first!

The Law of Attraction operates from thoughts, feelings, and beliefs. Often those beliefs are formed by the age of seven, and we are unaware that we even really feel that way. All a belief is, is someone else's idea that you've just kept on thinking. Beliefs quickly show up in your point of attraction as unwanted or unpleasant experiences. You may say to yourself; I would never ask for that in my life, but then you must think about your beliefs and challenge what you really know about yourself.

Let's say there is something about your current situation you want to change. We are all part of one unified energy field. In order to access that energy field, our frequency must be high. The frequency of pure energy is very high. A good and reliable way to raise your frequency is through meditation. Meditation allows you to travel internally, calm the nervous system, raise your frequency, and tap into the energy. When you're "tapped" in, you get insight, better clarity, and better timing. If the circumstance we wanted to change was that our kids were fighting and we wanted them to stop, the best way to go about stopping them is to raise your frequency. Everything pleasant, you've asked for through the living of life that takes place on a higher frequency. If your kids are arguing, then you must change frequencies and go to the frequency where they don't argue. Asking them not to argue while staying on the same frequency is like asking a tree to sit down.

## You Get What You Think About, Wanted or Not

Standing in the now and trying to change things is really hard, because you look around and you already see what's happening, but you have to keep in mind that your present reality is already manifested. You need to *feel* what you want to manifest in the future. If you look around yourself and just feel what's already in your life, you get more of the same. If there are things that are manifesting that you don't like, you have to ignore what is happening in your experience, or you will continue to get more of the same. You have to remember that like attracts like. Feelings have higher frequency than thought. As an example, if you are in the present moment and you are trying to manifest money because your bank account is overdrawn, but you keep saying to yourself, "I am rich, I am rich," it will still be very hard to manifest if you are feeling the scarcity of the overdrawn bank account. You have to completely withdraw from the feeling of the bank account and not only have thoughts about how much money you have, but also you have to *feel* what it would feel like to have that money.

I think of it like a bubble in my own mind when I get stuck on a concept. The bubble isn't empty, instead it has many floors. At the start of the day, you drive your bubble car to work. On your drive, if you don't know about the LOA, let's say you are tuned in to frequency 200. On bubble frequency 200, it's an average day. Birds are normal color, singing at a normal pitch, not over abundant. You have some traffic. Someone cuts you off and makes you mad. Now you are on bubble frequency 150. On bubble frequency 150, there is a bit more traffic. You see a policeman has someone pulled over on the side of the road, which makes you kind of irritated. You pull in to McDonald's for coffee. Someone could've let you in the line, but they didn't... bubble frequency 100. You order your food eventually. You pull away and notice they have made your coffee wrong. They forgot the hash browns. The momentum of the negative keeps continuing. Let's compare this to someone who does know about the LOA, who focuses on positive thought. They also start their day at bubble frequency 200. Birds are the same as above, again with some traffic. Someone cuts off our LOA driver but they don't get irritated. In fact, they like the song on the radio, dance a little bit, and their frequency goes up to 250. The traffic is lighter and it's easy to switch lanes. That makes you happy so your frequency goes up to 300. Our driver notices a police officer on the side of the highway helping someone change their tire. Frequency increase to 350. Our driver stops at McDonald's.

There is no wait, and he finds five dollars he forgot about in his wallet. The better it gets, the better it gets.

I have spent my entire life looking for happiness or waiting for the "next thing" to make me happy. It wasn't until I discovered that happiness is all an inside job that I freed everyone in my life from their eternal duty of pleasing me. My vibration is my job. The emotions live in me. I can visit them anytime I want. I can't be unhappy, waiting for happy to join me. My unhappy vibration won't even let the happy in. You get what you think about and what you feel, whether it is deliberate, or whether it is haphazard. I like to know that the things headed my way allow me to better understand where my point of attraction is at any given time so I have the opportunity to adjust.

In a practical example, let's consider your toddlers' sleep. In chapter 5, we examined the importance of a bedtime routine. This routine sets up your child's expectations. By adding this new information – you get what you think about – to what we already know, let's consider a scenario.

Your child is very aware of the bedtime routine, and you've been practicing the routine for a while. However, bedtime is still a hard time at your house. What else is there to consider? What are your thoughts regarding your toddlers sleep?

- My toddler never wants to go to bed.
- My toddler takes a long time to fall asleep.
- My child is a light sleeper.
- My child has never been a good sleeper.

If any of these resonate with you, it's time to change the story. Remember, your subconscious will give you exactly what you believe. It may take some time to change your patterns of belief when it comes to your child's sleep, but through practiced, habitual thought, you can change what you believe. When your thoughts regarding your child's sleeping habits switch to "My child sleeps great," your child *will* begin to sleep great!

## Guidance System

> *"if you're not excited about it, it's not the right path"*
> *-Abraham Hicks*

We are equipped with our own guidance system that tells us when we are headed in the right direction, vibrationally or not. Anytime we feel negative emotion, it means that the Source energy within us is not in the same place, so we feel the mis-alignment of it. Our one goal and purpose in life is to follow our happy. If it doesn't feel good, go the other way. If it feels good, keep going.

What does this have to do with your toddler? Consider your toddler your mirror. Since children are a source of pure positive energy, they are feeding you back exactly what your vibration is feeding them. If they are grumpy, it's because you're grumpy. If they won't eat their peas, maybe it's because your vibration is saying "I'm worried he won't eat his peas," or, "He's not going to like this." When you're crabby, the best idea is to find a way to get into alignment and then interact with your child, or else you will continue to get more of what you are getting. There is not enough action that will change the experience. Everything is vibration.

Pay attention to how your toddler acts around certain people. If you always have issues with your child when your mother or best friend is around, you can dive deeper. People often provide split energy and while they are happy to see your toddler, they may hate his screaming. In this Universe, you get what you think about. If your best friend is happy to see him, but visualizing your last experience when he was screaming, your child is picking up on that energy. The best thing for you to do in this scenario is to align with your energy and do your best to stay there. Remember, they can tell your frequency by how you feel. If you're feeling great, you have a higher frequency. If your friend or toddler wants to interact with you, they have to come to your frequency to do so. There is no assertion, only attraction! What happens on higher frequencies are the things that are most pleasing to you!

This work takes practice and commitment, but it will improve your life like nothing else! Mama, you have to take care of you first. If you don't take time to meditate and align, you will be on the hamster wheel your whole life. It is so much easier being guided with impulses from Source energy. You can't fill someone else's cup from an empty cup. Believe me, I've tried. You are everything to them. Give them a happy mom, and give yourself a happy mom.

# 9

## WHAT DO I DO WHEN A TANTRUM OCCURS NOW?

*"Yesterday I was clever, so I wanted to change the world. Today I am wise, so I am changing myself."*

*-Rumi*

### Creating Your Own Reality

My very first internal awareness that Law of Attraction (LOA) was more than just positive thinking hit me like a lightning bolt. I was sitting on my bed, and out of the blue, I profoundly understood LOA in a new way. These profound, understanding moments have happened to me several times over these past months, and I attribute them to a raise in vibration, which allows for "downloads" of information. When I understood LOA for the first time as more than a positive thinking approach, I hopped up off my bed, laughing hysterically, and yelled," I *literally create my own reality!*" I felt pure ecstasy, like nothing could stop me ever again. The fear was gone, the worry was gone, the overwhelming "something is going to happen to my kids" feeling was gone. I thought to myself, "I think I'll put money in the mailbox!" I ran downstairs, fully expecting it to be there! To my disappointment, it wasn't. I have studied LOA about every moment since then, and what I know for certain now is, finding money in the mailbox is possible, but it takes work.

It all comes down to belief (emotion) and expectation (absence of resistance). If your mom called you and said, "I think I'm going to send you money in the next coming year," feel how that feels versus if your mom called and said, "I put a check in the mail for you today." Feel the difference of the second statement, when you knew for certain that the check was on the way. When you feel that subtle shift in your emotion from thinking it's a possibility to knowing it's a sure deal, that's how you know your vibration has shifted.

Once I knew I had control over my reality, I thought it would be smooth sailing. I thought I wouldn't have a hard day, and life would be easy breezy. Well, that's not true, but I don't want you to get discouraged. Understanding energy is a game changer, but it does require focus, determination, and practice to work on your thinking. In this chapter, I want to highlight what to do when tantrums occur, now that you are aware of your vibrational nature.

## Becoming Aware of Your Point of Attraction

It's an early morning, and you've controlled as much as you possibly can by having things ready. There are no decisions to be made about clothes, since your two-year-old helped pick his clothes last night. You know exactly what you're making for breakfast. You have plenty of time, maybe ten minutes extra. You would never indulge anyone by sharing that secret, but you know you have a small buffer. The hard part is coming, the part you've been dreading. You know if you can put your toddler's shoes on, it will take two seconds, but you know that it's an almost impossible feat these days, with his independent streak. Here it comes – you brace yourself and tell him it's time for his shoes. You ask him to come over by you so you can put his shoes on. He yells that he is putting his shoes on. How could this happen when you've had such a great morning?

At any moment in time, you can tell vibrationally if you are in the right direction or not. If you are feeling good, you are in the right direction of Source energy. If you are feeling a negative emotion, you are feeling resistance. Any negative emotion is being cut off from the Source energy within you. *However, you will always get what you expect!* In the above example, because your expectation was that your two-year-old would have a problem with his shoes, he had a problem with his shoes. If you truly had the expectation that he would sit and behave while you put his shoes on, that's what would happen.

Every day, I am reminded of my point of attraction. I think, "Ok, today I am flying." Nothing unwanted will show up in my experience. Then, *bam*, there it is. It can be in the form of a grouchy child, a spouse that makes you feel underappreciated, a car that cuts you off, dog poop you step in. The list is endless.

However, this list provides you the opportunity to fine tune and become super clear about where you are. You can find beliefs that don't serve you. You can practice staying aligned, even when conditions aren't pleasant, and you can really zone in on the clarity you are seeking. If your day is not all ease and flow, your vibration is not all ease and flow. It makes it easier for me, if I'm having a moment, to concentrate on finding people smiling and laughing, because I know I am slowly raising my vibration to a place that allows happiness. Therefore, more happiness will naturally come into my experience.

If you can see energy – and you can – you can see that it is sticky. Place your hands up in front of you and soften your gaze while looking at your fingers. Don't look sharply at the end of your fingers, but instead look at all of your fingers for a few minutes. If you pay attention, you'll be able to discern what appears to be an outline around the edge of your hand and each finger. This outline is your aura. Now if you pull your fingers apart, or put your hands together and pull them apart, you'll notice this outline grows because it is pulling towards the energy it feels in the other hand or other finger. That is exactly how energy communicates. Different frequencies of energy clump together. That's how you attract. Your energy is pulling energy of the same frequency towards you. The opposite goes for different frequencies. Your energy is repelled from it. You don't create a frequency consistent with something until you truly, subconsciously believe it. If you would want to manifest money in your life, you would first have to emit a vibration that attracts money, and the only way to do that is to truly feel like you have money. If you can practice vibrating at the frequency (emotion) of anything, before that anything appears, then that anything you are wanting has to come in to your experience.

Rarely do people vibrate a frequency deliberately, so most often what ends up happening is a person looks around their present reality and emits a frequency based on what they see. That produces more of what they already have. You can tell exactly how someone feels about themselves by looking at their outer world. It is an exact vibrational match of their inner world. Most illnesses are long thought patterns of negative emotion that have years of momentum and have manifested in the body, and as you make yourself sick, you can also make yourself well. It's the same principle as above. You just have to have the belief and the expectation of wellness.

Everyone in your life is drawn to you by vibration. Your energies are pulled together. That's why you often find a connection and shared hobbies with people you meet, because you are on the same frequency. Family groups operate around the same frequency.

## Don't Let Negative Experiences Build Momentum

Nothing is more frustrating than hearing your child screaming and having a tantrum. First off, it doesn't mean you have failed, but you must quickly recover. Let the child be for a few minutes while you realign your own energy. If your energy is not realigned to a high frequency, what you do with your actions will be minute in comparison. There are some energy changing tips later in this chapter. Once you have realigned yourself, it is time to help your child realign. Remember, the longer the tantrum goes, the more steam it builds.

If you can sit close by *while keeping your energy up*, that is one way to bring him out of it. You can also engage with him, if you can keep your vibration steady. If your attention to him is going to bring you to his frequency, stay away until he is finished. It will take you both longer to recover.

The very best time to stop a tantrum is at the very beginning. Literally snap him out of it. Pinch his butt, make a silly face, jump in a puddle, anything. As soon as you can sense his energy shifting, change the momentum to the opposite direction. If he starts screaming because he wants candy in the store, whisper in his ear. He can't scream and listen at the same time. Whisper for him to find his nose, or look for something red. However, he cannot rationalize when he is upset. He will never understand why he cannot have candy. You can tell him about dinner, you can tell him about his teeth, he doesn't care. The insight here is that he is pure positive energy, already aligned and following his happy. What you are telling him is to dismiss his own guidance system and follow you. That is a big ask as a mother. Deciding where the line is, where the rules are. How much of your child's experience you let them create for themselves. Children are powerful creators, it is the adults that haphazardly use their magic wands.

As mothers, we want to always make sure our children are happy. However, your three-year-old will control your behavior with a tantrum in order to get what they want. That is not the kind of happy we are responsible for giving. We can wish and want for them to be happy, but we cannot or should not try to control if they are happy. You will be held captive by your child's screams in order to have their demands met. You have to teach people how to treat you, and that includes your child. If you are non-responsive to a tantrum, they will see it as an ineffective problem-solving method.

## Energy Changing Ideas

As soon as you notice that your frequency is not where you want it to be, your first priority should be trying to get back into alignment with Source energy. Regardless of what you try, action wise, it will be miniscule in comparison to just tending to your energy. Here are some quick ideas to help get your frequency raised.

- Meditate. Mediation stops negative thought, which brings you back to a neutral space. In that neutral space, without the inflection of your negative thoughts, your frequency will automatically rise.
- Have an impromptu dance party. This is great for turning the energy around. Turn the music up loud! Act silly, get your kids involved! They will love it, and in no time, you will be feeling better!
- Write a list of things you are grateful for and all of the things going well in your life.
- Go outside in nature. Look around, appreciate everything around you.
- Look out the window. Acknowledge a Source greater than yourself, and become aware and appreciate that the universe has your back and is looking out for you.
- Exercise for a few minutes, even if its just running up and down a flight of stairs for a few minutes.
- Stand up and yell, move the energy in a different direction. Be silly while yelling. Shake your body out.
- Call a positive friend and tell them something you love about them.

- Send an email to someone, and list all of the things you appreciate about them.
- Hug your child, and then tickle them unexpectedly.
- Go on a bike ride.
- Do something you know makes you calm! I like to vacuum when my energy is low, but if you hate vacuuming, then don't do it!
- Appreciate the flowers outside. Walk through your flower bed, and pick out which flower is your favorite. Tell the flower it is your favorite.
- Listen to your favorite music.
- Spend five minutes looking up something on the internet that you enjoy.
- Make a list of ten things that you think are awesome about your child.
- Make a list of ten things that you think are awesome about yourself.

Quick activities you enjoy doing will help slow or stop negative thoughts. Your natural state is a high frequency. All you have to do is control the negative emotion from creeping in. The fantastic part is you have complete control over your life. It may seem circumstances come to you, and you have a reaction. In this universe, there is no assertion. Absolutely no one can create in your experience that you are not a vibrational match to. Do you know how much power that gives you, if you own it and step into that power? When you become the creator, you were born to be, you will learn to see things through the eyes of Source with unconditional love. Our love, as humans, is conditional. "If you do this, and it pleases me, I will love you." Unconditional love is loving someone through their poor choices, without judgment. If you can move a step closer to your bliss every day, think of where you will be in a year from now. How rich will your life be? When you put love into the universe, only love can come back.

# 10

# TAKING THE FIRST STEPS

*"we cannot become what we want*
*by remaining what we are"*
*-Max Depree*

You have some ideas now, but the concept of making lifelong lasting changes may still feel overwhelming. If you could turn off the lights for a minute, set everything up, go to retreat for thirty days, figure out how to do all of the internal work, come back, reset, and then turn everything back on and start right where you left off, *then* it might be easy.

Obviously, in the real world, change has to take place simultaneously with living your life. Every small step in the right direction is a great step. It's going to feel like some days you're getting nowhere. Don't give up. You're exactly where you need to be. Be easy on yourself.

## Cost of Giving Up

If you give up completely, your days are out of control again and filled with exhaustion, chaos, and lack of clarity. Your toddler loses too. Because his limits are shaky, he's not hearing his own internal guidance, and your guidance to him is inconsistent, based on your reaction to him. If you're having a hard day, it's just reminding you where your point of attraction is. Thank the Universe for the reminder.

Remember, you're in control. You can stop the ball rolling down the hill. Do one of the energy changing ideas to get your frequency back up, and you will see your point of attraction start to change. I know, this takes work and focus. As soon as you notice anything in the correct direction, acknowledge it. Be grateful it has shown up. More will show up for you. If you can't get it back in the moment, the momentum will stop when you sleep; however, you must consciously choose new thoughts in the morning.

You *can* have it all: the control in your life, the happy family, the happiness for yourself. My wish for you is that you discover your worthiness and your value. You see how capable you are and how easily you can manage your family situation. It's *your* thoughts that keep you trapped and limited, nothing else. You are only trapped by thoughts that you have continued to think! Stop thinking the thoughts that keep you limited!

You found this book to find help with your toddler. Consider what happens if everything remains the same. What brought you to this book? What was keeping you up at night? What if you just go back to living the same way you were before reading this book? How will your relationship with your toddler look in six months? How will your relationship with yourself look in six months?

On the other hand, think about what peace and control over your life would look and feel like. Think about waking up and being excited to start the day.

## Tantrum Checklist

Go through the list of steps. Start with the external environment you've created. Ask yourself *"what caused this tantrum?"*

1. Planning and preparation
   - Is it planning? If you could've planned better, you've learned for next time.
   - Does my child have engaging activities?
   - Did I stop my child's activity without warning?
   - Are you using a transition timer?
   - Did the tantrum occur when we were not home?

If the problem was not in planning and preparation, move on to trust and security.

2. Trust and Security
   - Is my child feeling secure in his external environment?
   - Do I have clear limits?
     - Are they too rigid?
     - Do they allow for playfulness?
   - Did I take away my child's control by taking him out of his routine?
   - Was this a hungry or tired time for my child?
   - Was this a problem at bedtime?
     - Do I have a clear bedtime routine in place?

If you have not been able to identify what created the tantrum, go through the next set of questions.

3. Am I present for my child? Am I kind when I speak to my child?

- Is the problem me?
  - o Am I distracted when my child is trying to speak to me?
  - o Is my mood consistent with my child?
- Am I sending my child mixed messages?
- Is this a discipline or conscious parenting issue?
  - o Could I have been more proactive in preventing what occurred, therefore alleviating the need for discipline?

If you are sure you are staying present and being kind, check the following.

4. Going Within
   - What are my thoughts?
   - Do I have momentum in a negative direction?
     - o Would meditation help clear my mind?
   - Am I worried about something?

If you've identified negative thoughts or momentum, it's time for energy changing ideas or meditation. If you have not been able to identify negative thoughts or emotions, ask yourself the following questions.

5. Self-Awareness
   - What is my vibrational nature?
   - What is showing up in my experience? Is everything light and easy? Remember, you attract everything to you. If you are seeing anything in your current reality that is not pleasant, you are emitting a vibration that is allowing it into your experience.
     - o Is it all ease and flow?

- Did I let a negative experience gain momentum?
- Have I tried to change my energy frequency?

If you've identified that the problem is your vibration, you must snap out of it. Start with your emotional guidance system. What emotion are you feeling? You cannot get from worried to happy immediately, but we have to turn the direction of your thoughts. Pick any subject that feels better and purposely guide your thoughts there for one minute, until they gain some momentum. With that new thought, after one minute, pick another thought that feels a little bit better. Purposefully concentrate on that for one minute.

## A Real Life Example

Let me give you an example how to go through the checklist to identify the problem.

I hate the mornings, especially school mornings. If it were up to me, all days would start at noon. Every morning during the school year, I would have my own two children, who were eight and ten at the time, who I would need to pack lunches for and get breakfast. In addition to them, I had a two-year-old, a three-year-old, and a four-year-old. One morning, I could hear the three-year-old and four-year-old fighting about a toy. I continued to pack lunches because I was running out of time. The three-year-old then decided to hit the four-year-old, so now, they were both crying. I yelled at my children to put their tablets away and finish getting ready for school.

Let's examine the above scenario. First, going through the list, I had poor planning. I could've packed lunches the night before, but I chose to do it in the morning. Second, the young children are playing in the toy room, but I do not have any engaging activities for them to interact with. So, with planning, I have identified two hot spots that I could improve on. I should've packed lunches the night before, and I should've had an engaging table activity.

Now, let's move on through trust and security. Are my limits clear? Not necessarily. For the young children that morning, I have not provided any limits, nor have I provided any structure to their external environment. For improvement, I could've told them I was setting the timer, and when they hear it go off, it means it's time for breakfast. Then they would have predictability and feel some control.

Was I present and kind? No. If I had been present in the moment, I would not have been distracted making lunches. This would've allowed me, through conscious parenting, to step in before fighting occurred. I would've been able to anticipate it because of the growing escalation. I also was not kind, because I was distracted and rushed, I yelled at my own two children, who I should've been more present and proactive with.

Moving on, let's continue to see how my thoughts affected this scenario. I already said I hated the morning. When you open yourself up to thoughts of "I hate this activity," more reasons of why you hate it will add on to the first thought. I could've changed my thoughts to how productive mornings can be. Just changing the thought about mornings will change my entire experience of how mornings feel.

Lastly, in my experience, I have children who are not ready on schedule, children fighting over toys, and a lack of time. I could tell my vibration is not ease and flow. In order to get myself back to a better frequency, I can try any of the energy changing ideas. To set myself up for a better morning, I should've also meditated when I first awakened. This would've allowed me to start at a higher frequency, and I could've avoided a tough morning all together.

## Continued Support

Imagine you found out it was your last day on earth. You couldn't have any thoughts about what would happen tomorrow because there would be no tomorrow. Think about your interactions with people throughout the day, and how it would be different from your interactions with people on a normal day. Think about your interactions with your child on your last day on earth. Think about how it would feel to listen to music for the last time. Think about what it would look like to look at the sky, or the stars, or the moon, if you knew it was going to be your last time. How you would look at them differently?

That is what living in the present feels like, where there is no thought of the future and there is no thought in the past. Your child is playing that way every single day. They are not concerned about the future, they are not concerned who is going to pay the mortgage, or the phone bill. Stay in that world with your child, because that is the world we are meant to live in. From that world, you will find the energy and creativity necessary to be the most dynamic and exciting mother that you ever thought possible. If you need help re-finding that world or you keep falling out, I can help you find your secret door back.

Think how much easier this process would be if you had a daily plan in place and knew you would be successful every day. You're a busy mom. I wish you every success in finding peace in your life. I hope these ideas are easy for you to implement, and your toddler responds quickly. Nothing is more important to me than letting mothers feel their worthiness and value so they can pass that on to their children. There truly is no other job like being a mother. That being said, in order to ensure your success, I want to make it as easy as possible.

My wish for you is that you take this information, that it is applicable in your life, and you are able to easily adopt the strategies provided. Consciously living and parenting in a different way takes practice and support. I invite you to join my email list for follow up questions and group discussions. There, you will be able to ask specific questions about your child. I offer my support to you because I know it is a life-long process, and as you step into your worthiness, some people may drift away. I offer my support to you because it's your time, your turn to understand the magical wonder of the world, and to help you share the gift with your own children.

# 11

## FOLLOW YOUR HAPPY

*"In the end, I am the only one who can give my*
*daughter a happy mother who loves life"*
*-author unknown*

I wrote this book because I wanted mothers, who have the most thankless job but give the most of themselves, to know that within their worthiness lies the secret to life's wishes. I wrote this book so another mother doesn't have to question her value and wait for someone to notice how much effort she's put in before she feels good about herself. I wrote this book, so mothers realize their happiness and love is all inside, and the peace they are seeking in their outer world comes from finding peace in their inner world. I wrote this book so other mothers don't judge themselves against societal standards, but instead judge themselves based on whether or not they are happy enough.

The feeling that tells you, "You're not good enough," is from you. It is only a habit of thought that you have continued to think. It is a belief that you've chosen for yourself because you allow yourself to make comparisons of what you think you have to offer based on a societal standard. You don't have to live that way anymore. You are good enough. The subconscious requires habitual thinking, and it's time to change your story. My wish for you mamas is to be able to maintain a peaceful environment for yourself and step into your own worthiness.

## Final Recap

To prevent tantrums, we went from work on the external environment to work on the internal environment.

### External Work

- Start planning and prepping activities that are quick, ready to get out, and that the child doesn't normally see.
- Create routines and follow through. This makes your child feel control in their environment and allows them to know what is coming.
- Learn the importance of transitioning out of activities.

### Internal Work

- Stay present and be kind. Being mindful can bring a child away from a tantrum immediately, and there are benefits of kindness.
- Start with meditation, types of meditation, and benefits of meditation.
- Develop self-awareness and realize of your point of attraction.
- Use the checklist to learn what to do when tantrums occur. Use these tips for mom to help toddler stay out of tantrum or get toddler out of tantrum as soon as possible.

The steps outlined in this book will make a big difference in your life. You should be able to enjoy motherhood. You have the privilege of caring for souls also on their Earth journey. Realize life is magical, and your children come through you, not to you. Be the best guide you can.

I want you to realize there are no merits given out for self-sacrifice. I watched my mother and my friends' mothers and mothers on TV give all of themselves to their families. Maybe it was easier when families could survive on one income, but whole-hearted self-sacrifice and the demands of life are nearly impossible to get through without mental illness. Motherhood is not about giving up your health, your comfort, your happiness, your well-being to care for others. When you've sacrificed everything of yourself, you have nothing left for yourself. Full self-sacrifice feels like prison. If you don't ever make choices for yourself, how long can you maintain that state of being before resentment sets in?

Motherhood is about self-care first. It's about setting your vibrational atmosphere so only good things come your way. Motherhood is about showing your children how to treat you by the way you treat yourself and by the way you treat them. It's not how much you sacrifice for them. They don't understand. They want the whole you. The better you.

What's going on in your outside world is exactly what is going on in your inside world. You cannot attract a vibration you aren't emitting. There is no assertion. A frequency not on your vibration cannot "pop" into your experience. When you understand that, it sets you free from letting anyone else determine how you feel. If you don't like how someone is talking to you, you're emitting it from them. Happiness attracts happiness, calm attracts calm.

Don't let other people's happiness flow through you. Do not teach your children that their happiness comes from you. This starts you on a cycle of self-sacrifice and prevents your child from learning how to be responsible for their emotions. Teach your child how to use their own emotions as a guide. When things are tough, show them they can find anything that feels better to think about and follow it. Continue to follow better feeling emotions. In no time, they too, will be able to follow their own bliss.

Mama, the most important thing is that no one can tell you how to feel. You can always reach for something that feels better. If the subject you're thinking about is not allowing you to find a thought to feel good about, change the subject. When you decide you want to feel good regardless of what anyone else says or does, you have *complete* control over your life.

Mothering a toddler should and can be fun. It is a time when children are picking up so much information, and the world is coming alive again through their eyes! It is so fun to experience things again for the first time through your toddler's eyes! Don't waste this time bound up in anger and pity surrounded by stares from strangers and screams from your child. You deserve better, and you can have better!

I know when I first learned and understood the vibrational nature of the world, I wanted to shout it from the rooftops! You want everyone you love to benefit from your understanding. At first, I wrote an email to my entire family explaining it the best I could, then I would try to explain it individually. Their "not" getting it would throw me out of my vibration every single time.

I have learned that if they are not open to receive the information, they will not receive it. You are not on Earth to make sure other humans understand your journey in life. Their souls will open when they're supposed to. For now, practice feeling good and let the universe amaze you!

You don't have to make yourself sick to be a great mother, you have to make yourself happy! There is no other work for you to do other than to be happy. Watch how much better life starts to get. When you realize you control all of your own switches about what is true in your reality and not your past beliefs or ideas or society or your neighbor or your mother or your toddler you will only scratch the surface of the literal true power you hold! You would then see there is no reason to hold on to any belief that does not let you live the exact life you want to live.

# ACKNOWLEDGMENTS

To all of the two-year olds who have meandered through my life, I have learned so much. To Marc, Sara, Laura, Tyler my first two-year olds. To Jane, Avonlea, Adam, Owen, Peter, Ozzie, Hunter, Isaac, Jinaan, Logan, Scarlett, Morgan, Rhetty, Vaida, Nellie, Liv and Jaxon. To my parents, Charlyne and Earl for always loving me and showing me the way. Thank you for trusting me even when I think I could fail. Thank you for always believing in the best outcome. To Jesse for believing in me when I didn't believe in myself. To Mark for listening to my magic stories and always having my back. To the teachers I've had along the way, thank you for opening the door.

Thank you to Angela Lauria and The Author Incubator's team for helping me bring this book to print.

# THANK YOU

Thank you so much for reading My Toddler Has Stopped Having So Many Tantrums. I know if you read this book your toddler was driving you crazy! It is your turn to experience the peace and bliss that life has to offer. Build a future that feels exciting!

I would love to be able to share in this journey with you as you move forward. I can easily be reached at stoptoddlertantrums@gmail.com. It has been a pleasure writing this book for you and look forward to hearing from you in the future!

# ABOUT THE AUTHOR

Susan Jungermann lives with her two children in Dublin, Ohio and has spent the last twenty years focusing on child development, specifically with toddlers, while using her degree in early childhood education. Running a childcare center, Susan had constant chaos in her life and needed to find a way to stop all of the toddler tantrums. In doing so, she discovered a way to bring peace and happiness to her inner and outer world.